MW01121000

Building the Erie Canal

Rebecca Stefoff

Cavendish
Square

New York

Published in 2018 by Cavendish Square Publishing, LLC
243 5th Avenue, Suite 136, New York, NY 10016

Library of Congress Cataloging-in-Publication Data

Names: Stefoff, Rebecca, 1951- author.
Title: Building the Erie Canal / Rebecca Stefoff.
Description: New York : Cavendish Square Publishing, 2018. | Series: Engineering North America's landmarks | Includes bibliographical references and index.
Identifiers: LCCN 2017016784 (print) | LCCN 2017023043 (ebook) | ISBN 9781502629630 (E-book) | ISBN 9781502629609 (pbk.) | ISBN 9781502629623 (library bound) | ISBN 9781502629616 (6 pack)
Subjects: LCSH: Erie Canal (N.Y.)--History--Juvenile literature.
Classification: LCC TC625.E6 (ebook) | LCC TC625.E6 S74 2018 (print) | DDC 627/.13809747--dc23
LC record available at https://lccn.loc.gov/2017016784

Editorial Director: David McNamara
Editor: Fletcher Doyle
Copy Editor: Rebecca Rohan
Associate Art Director: Amy Greenan
Designer: Alan Sliwinski
Production Coordinator: Karol Szymczuk
Photo Research: J8 Media

Printed in the United States of America

Contents

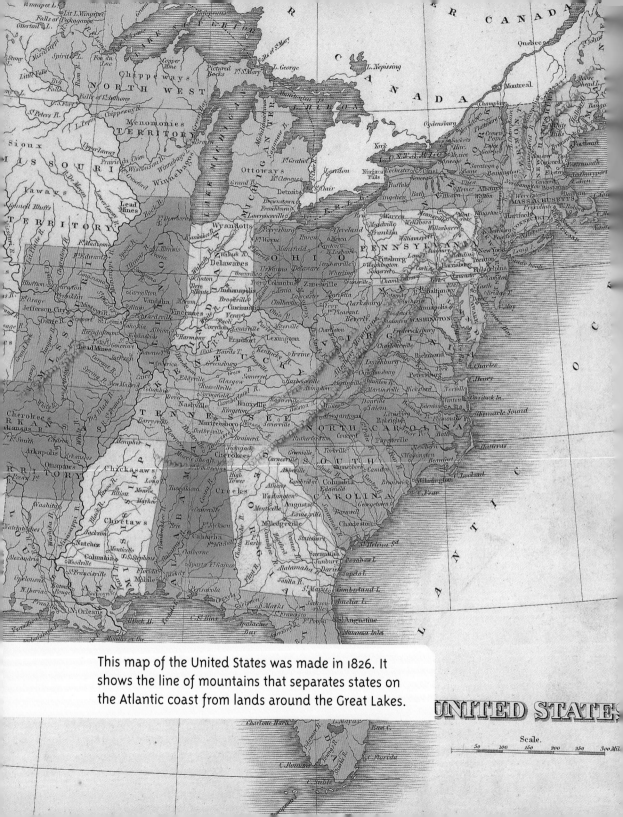

This map of the United States was made in 1826. It shows the line of mountains that separates states on the Atlantic coast from lands around the Great Lakes.

UNITED STATES

Scale.

50   100   150   200   250   300 Mil.

Chapter One

Needed: A New Way West

I n the year 1800, the United States was a young country. However, it was growing. Most of its people lived near the Atlantic Ocean. Many of them wanted to settle new land.

This land was to the west. It was in the area near the Great Lakes. There was just one problem. Getting there wasn't easy. Solving that problem would take a big idea. It would need lots of hard work.

The Long Road West

Railroads didn't exist. People traveled westward in wagons. Mule trains pulled goods for trade or sale.

It was a rough journey. Roads were bad. Forests covered the land. The Appalachian Mountains stood in the way.

People traveled west in wagon trains. The wagons carried supplies. Most people walked.

Travel was slow. It took two-and-a-half weeks
to go from New York City to Cleveland, Ohio. Only
fifty-seven people lived in Cleveland in 1807.

What About Water?

The easiest way to travel then was by water. Boats
carried people and goods much faster than wagons.

The harbor at New York City around 1838 was already busy. The early United States
depended on water to move people and goods quickly.

Ships and boats moved from city to city along the coast. In the Midwest, boats traveled on the Ohio and Mississippi Rivers. They sailed on the Great Lakes. However, there was no way to get from the coast to those rivers and lakes by water.

Countries such as Great Britain and France were digging **canals**. A canal is a channel made by people to carry water. Canals can connect rivers

In 1807, a steamboat carried passengers on the Hudson River from Albany to New York and back in sixty-two hours.

and lakes. They even run between oceans. They make waterways for shipping. Some Americans wanted the United States to build a canal.

A New Idea

In 1808, the New York government decided to build a canal across the state. The eastern end would be in New York's capital city of Albany. It is on the Hudson River. The western end would be in the town of Buffalo on Lake Erie.

Americans had never built anything like it before. It would be a challenge.

Erie Canal by the Numbers

Time of construction: July 4, 1817, to October 26, 1825

Canal enlarged: 1836 to 1862

The route of the Erie Canal, which runs between Lake Erie and the Hudson River north of Albany

Elevation change: 680 feet (207 meters)

Length: 363 miles (584 km)

Depth: 4 feet (1.2 m) when new, 12–14 feet (3.6–4.2 m) today

Width: 40 feet (12 m) when new, 120 feet (36.6 m) today

Number of locks: 83 when new, 36 today

Cost: $7 million (about $163 million in today's dollars)

DeWitt Clinton, governor of
New York, made the canal a reality.

Chapter Two

Building the Canal

Three things were needed to build the Erie Canal. One was money. One was a **design.** The third was people to do the work. DeWitt Clinton, the governor of New York, got the money from the state by 1817. By then, a design was ready.

The Canal Design

Part of the Erie Canal would run next to the Mohawk River. This river starts near Lake Ontario.

It flows to the Hudson River. It passes through a valley in the Appalachian Mountains.

The canal would use the Mohawk River valley to get through the mountains. Then it would turn west to Lake Erie.

Planners knew that digging a canal would not be enough. They also had to build a firm path along the canal. This would let teams of horses and mules pull boats along the canal.

Going Uphill

The biggest problem was geography. The eastern end of the canal route is at sea level. This is the same level as the ocean. Its western end is more than 600 feet (183 m) higher. How would boats go up and down hills? Canal planners solved this problem with **aqueducts** and **locks.**

An aqueduct is a raised channel. It is built to carry water above land around it. It is like a canal that is also a bridge. A lock is a chamber that can be filled with water and then emptied. Boats in the chamber can be raised or lowered.

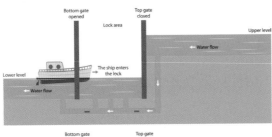

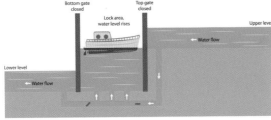

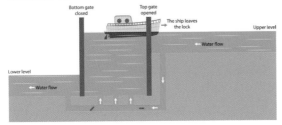

A lock is like an elevator for ships. A ship enters the lock from the lower level (*top*). Water fills the lock, raising the ship (*middle*). The ship can then sail out on the upper level (*bottom*). The same steps in reverse will lower a ship.

Engineers and Laborers

There were two main kinds of

workers on the Erie Canal. There were **engineers** and laborers.

Engineers make plans and see that things are built well. They use math and science. They invent technology. Engineers who work on public projects such as canals are called **civil engineers.**

Laborers used derricks made of timber and rope to carry away loads of dirt from the digging. Derricks were also used to lower loads of stones for lining the canal walls.

America did not have many civil engineers in the early 1800s. The main planners of the Erie Canal were two judges and a math teacher. They learned civil engineering on the job.

The canal project also needed laborers. The laborers cut down trees. They pulled up stumps. They moved boulders. Then they dug the channel and lined it with clay and stone. Laborers also built bridges and tunnels.

Thousands of men worked on the canal. Many came from Ireland. Laborers worked from dawn to dark.

Fast Fact

Workers on the canal were paid 50 to 80 cents a day. They were given meals and a place to sleep. They worked six days a week.

Building the canal was dangerous. Disease and accidents killed many laborers. Few people worked on the canal from start to finish.

Rising to Challenges

The engineers and the workers followed the plan. They built one section of the canal at a time. They built aqueducts over creeks and valleys. They built locks where the canal had to go up or down a hill. The locks moved the water and boats. Locks were stacked on long slopes like steps.

The last part of the canal had to be blasted through a ridge of rock. Some workers were killed by gunpowder.

The Erie Canal took eight years to build. It was finished in 1825.

Canvass White's Discovery

Canvass White studied math and science. He learned **surveying**. The United States lacked engineers. When he was twenty-six years old, he was sent to England. He was sent to learn how to build canals. He learned about tools and **cement**. In 1818, White made a discovery. He found a new limestone rock near Chittenango, New York. Limestone is used in cement. Chittenango limestone did not have to dry to become hard. It could harden underwater. The limestone made **hydraulic cement**. It is waterproof. Now New York would not have to buy cement from England.

White's cement replaced wood in locks. Wood rots when it stays wet. Hydraulic cement also plugged leaks in the walls of the canal.

When the Erie Canal opened, crowds cheered as the first boats traveled on America's new waterway.

Chapter Three

On the Erie Canal

When the Erie Canal was finished, the people of New York State knew it was a historical moment. They cheered and fired cannons along the canal for ninety minutes.

The Erie Canal was praised as an engineering wonder. Cities and towns grew along its banks. Tourists from many countries came to ride boats on it.

The canal helped make New York City much wealthier. Many goods were moved on the canal.

At an event called "The Marriage of Waters," DeWitt Clinton poured water from Lake Erie into the Atlantic Ocean.

This turned New York into the country's busiest port. Many people got jobs at the port. The canal also gave America a new waterway to the west.

Faster and Cheaper

A trip from Albany to Buffalo on the Erie Canal took about half the time as the same trip in a stagecoach. Goods could move quickly from the Great Lakes to New York City and then to Europe. Boats carried grain from farms. They moved timber from forests. There was coal from mines and minerals like salt. It cost much less to ship goods on canal boats than in wagons.

New York City was a center of banking and trade. The canal helped its port grow. By 1840, it was the country's biggest port. Buffalo grew from a town of a few hundred people to a bustling city. It became a major Great Lakes port. Other cities grew along the canal.

Moving People

The Erie Canal connected the center of America to the East Coast. Thousands of settlers went west on the canal. From Buffalo, they could travel on the Great Lakes. They could reach the Mississippi River by boat. Many were immigrants.

In George Harvey's painting *Pittsford on the Erie Canal* (1837), passengers enjoy the view from a packet boat. The boat is being pulled by three horses.

Goods were carried on barges. People traveled the canal on packet boats. Many passengers were tourists. Riding the canal was a sightseeing craze. As many as forty thousand people rode it in its first year.

The Erie Canal Today

The golden age of the Erie Canal began to end when railroads were built across New York State.

By 1842, the railroad line was finished. Passengers turned to this faster form of travel. Barges still carried goods on the canal. During the nineteenth century, the canal was made wider and deeper. New channels were cut.

Between 1902 and 1918, New York State replaced the original Erie Canal with the Barge Canal. The new canal used some sections of the old canal. Freight barges used the Barge Canal until the 1950s. It then became cheaper to move goods by train and truck.

Today, the Barge Canal is sometimes called the Erie Canal. Some cargo barges use it. So do tour boats and recreational boats. People also boat on sections of the original Erie Canal. They ride bikes on the towpath.

The Erie Canal was a heroic feat of engineering. Today, it is honored for its place in American history.

World's Five Longest Canals

1. Grand Canal, China. Created: 486 BCE to around 1280 CE. Length: 1,104 miles (1,776 km) from Beijing to Hangzhou. For: shipping.

2. Karakum Canal, Turkmenistan. Created: 1954–1988. Length: 854 miles (1,375 km) from Amu-Darya River to Karakum Desert. For: farming.

3. Erie Canal, United States. Created: 1817–1825. Length: 363 miles (584 km). For: shipping.

4. Grand Union Canal, Great Britain. Created: 1894–1929. Length: 286 miles (460 km). For: shipping.

5. Nara Canal, Pakistan. Created: 1932–1990. Length: 226 miles (364 km) from Indus River to Thar Desert. For: farming.

Erie Canal Quiz

1. The Erie Canal was built to connect what two bodies of water?

2. What was the biggest problem faced by the builders of the canal?

3. How did the Erie Canal climb up and down hills?

4. What replaced the Erie Canal?

Answers

1. The Hudson River and Lake Erie

2. Geography

3. Aqueducts and locks

4. The Barge Canal

Glossary

aqueduct A human-made channel for water that rises above the land around it.

canal A human-made water channel that may be large enough for ships to travel on it.

cement A material that hardens when it is dry. It is made of lime and clay.

civil engineer An engineer who works on public projects, such as dams and canals.

design A picture of how a finished project or product will look. It comes with a plan for how to build it or make it.

engineer Someone who uses science, math, and tools to build things.

hydraulic cement A kind of cement that can harden under water and stay waterproof.

lock A waterproof chamber that can be filled with water or drained. Boats in the lock go up or down with the water.

surveying Measuring the shape of piece of land so a map or engineering plan can be drawn.

Find Out More

Books

Drake, Patricia. *New York's Erie Canal*. New York: PowerKids Press, 2014.

Laplante, Walter. *The Erie Canal*. New York: Gareth Stevens, 2016.

Websites

The Erie Canal

www.eriecanal.org

This site is about the history of the Erie Canal. It includes many old pictures of how the canal was built and the boats that traveled on it in the early years.

Erie Canalway: A National Treasure

www.eriecanalway.org/learn/history-culture

This National Park Service site talks about the history, nature, and science of the Erie Canal.

📍 Index

Page numbers in **boldface** are illustrations. Entries in **boldface** are glossary terms.

About the Author

Rebecca Stefoff has written books for young readers on many topics in science, technology, and history. She is the author of the six-volume series Great Engineering (2016), the six-volume series Is It Science? (Cavendish Square, 2014), and the four-volume series Animal Behavior Revealed (Cavendish Square, 2014). She also wrote *The Telephone*, *The Camera*, *Submarines*, *The Microscope and Telescope*, and *Robots* for the Cavendish Square Great Inventions series. Stefoff lives in Portland, Oregon.